Kids Body Connection

Get Ready

1. Listen to Your Body
- eyes are looking
- ears are listening
- hands are down and still
- feet are down and still

2. Body Alignment

3. Soft Gaze

4. Box Breathing

IN — HOLD — OUT — HOLD

BOX Breathing

move it The Star

★ Tilting Star

★ Twirling Star

★ Twisting Star

Leah's Pantry Copyright | Pilot Materials

move it

WARM-UP

Flying Friends

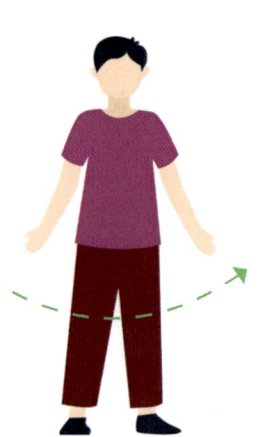

| Eagle | Hummingbird | Butterfly |

Neck Rolls

Stay Strong

Tightrope

Slingwater

The Shakes

The Triangle

Leah's Pantry Copyright | Pilot Materials

Kids Body Connection

NERVOUS SYSTEM

Did you know that beyond the five senses (touch, sight, smell, hearing, and taste) that give us information about the outside world, our nervous system also has receptors giving us insight into what is happening inside and around our bodies?

When we are stressed we might experience...

1. Tunnel Vision
2. Dry Mouth
3. Increased Breathing
4. Increased Heart Rate
5. Increased Glucose Release
6. Slowed Digestion
7. Release of Adrenaline
8. Contraction and Spasm
9. Constriction

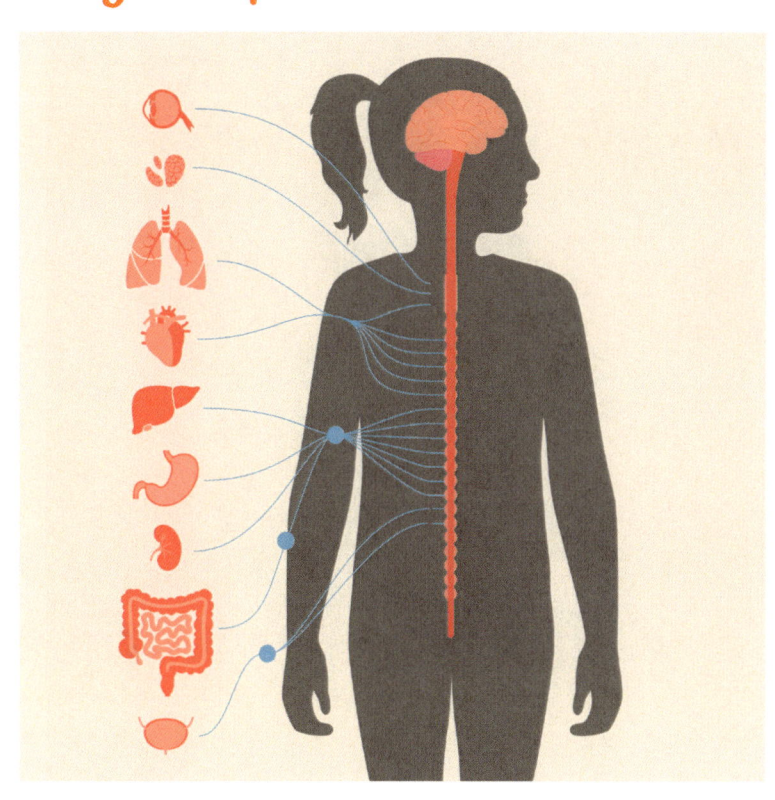

Healthy Fats
Improve your mood with food!

Eggs, olive oil, fish, seeds and nuts are great sources of "good" or healthy fats. These are among the many foods that have been shown to improve the health of our nervous systems.

Leah's Pantry Copyright | Pilot Materials

move it
Dance With the 6th & 7th Senses

NERVOUS SYSTEM

PROPRIOCEPTION
The 6th Sense

- judge distance
- move without looking
- avoid bumping into stuff
- move fluidly
- use the appropriate force

INTEROCEPTION
The 7th Sense

- feel how deep the breath is
- feel heart rate
- feel if need to pee
- feel hunger and fullness
- feel muscle tension

Tapping

Tap under your **eyes** to release your **INNER SMILE**

Tap on your **clavicles** to open your **HEART**

Tap on your **wrists** to relax your **HANDS**

Tap the **CROWN** of your head

Tap on your **temples** for **LASER VISION**

Tap **armpits to your hips** to activate your **SUPER POWERS**

Leah's Pantry Copyright | Pilot Materials

Kids Body Connection

RESPIRATORY SYSTEM

Breath is life! Inhaling oxygen kick starts the process that turns food into energy, with our cells utilizing the oxygen traveling through our lungs.

The respiratory system includes:

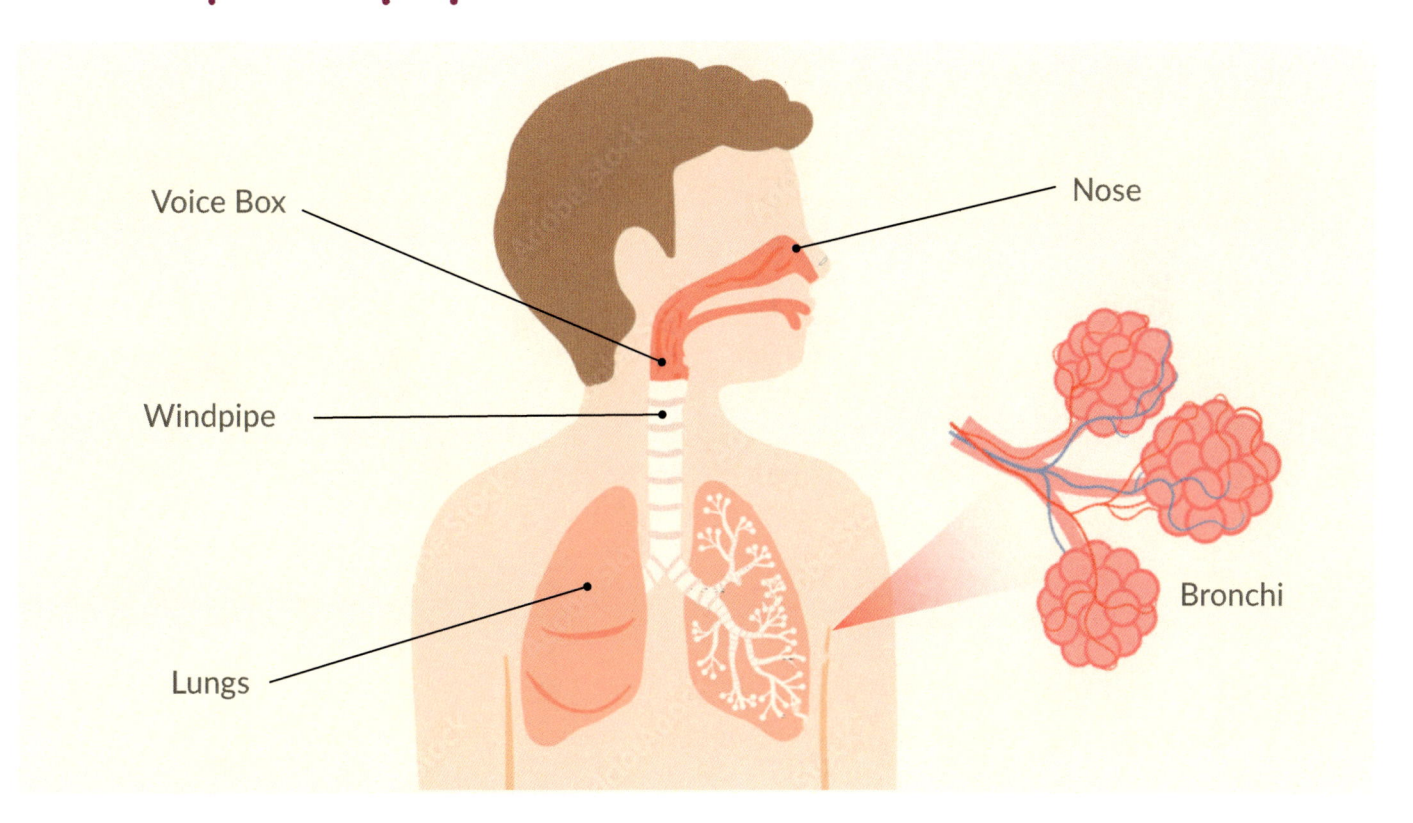

- Voice Box
- Nose
- Windpipe
- Lungs
- Bronchi

Spice it up!

Seasonings like onions, ginger, garlic, cinnamon and cilantro have amazing smells and flavors and they help circulatory and respiratory health.

FUN FACT!

The left lung is slightly smaller and has a notch to give room for the heart.

Leah's Pantry Copyright | Pilot Materials

move it

Whole Body Breathing

RESPIRATORY SYSTEM

1. Breathe in through your nose.
2. Breathe out through your mouth.

Bunny Breathing

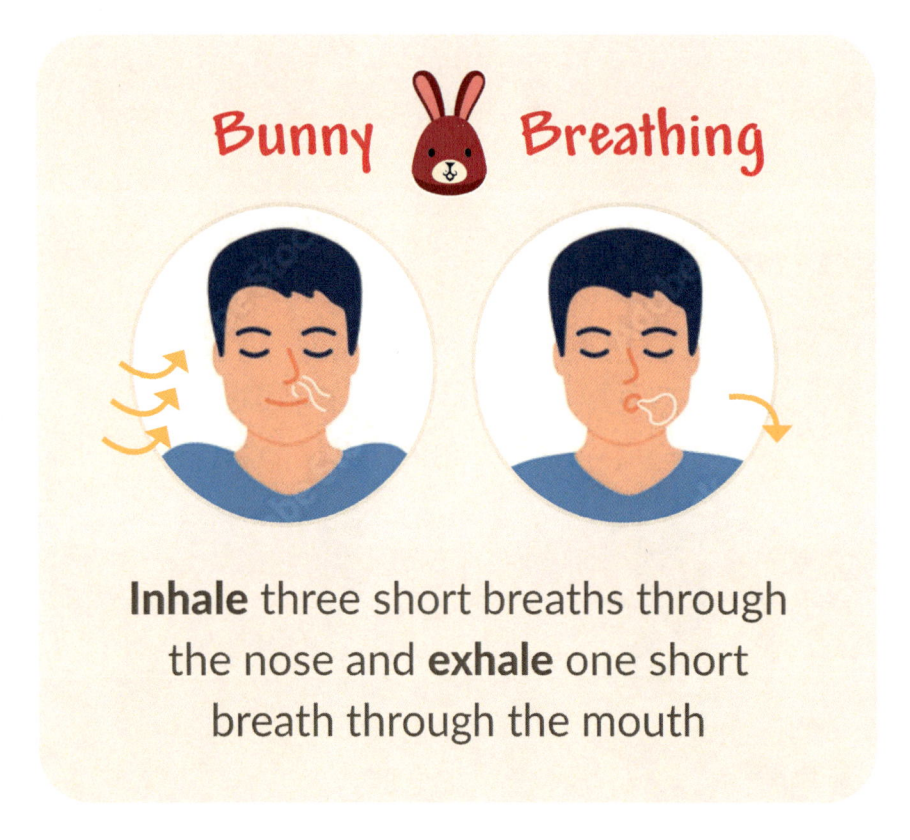

Inhale three short breaths through the nose and **exhale** one short breath through the mouth

Belly Breathing

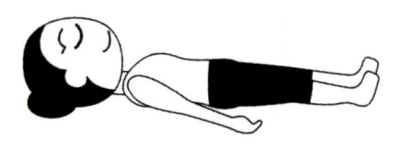

1. Start by relaxing all the muscles in your body.
2. Slowly take a deep breath in, filling your lungs with air. Your belly will fill up like a balloon. 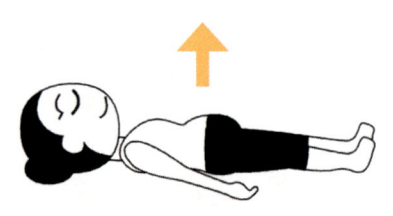
3. Slowly breathe out, squeezing all the air out of your belly balloon. Then repeat. 

Breath is life!

Leah's Pantry Copyright | Pilot Materials

Kids Body Connection

CARDIOVASCULAR SYSTEM

Did you know that your heart is an organ that is made of mostly muscle? Your heart acts like a pump, beating slower when resting and faster when moving.

How does the cardiovascular system work?

Ever wonder how oxygen and nutrients reach your cells and organs? It's through your cardiovascular system which consists of your **heart** and **blood vessels**.

When you inhale, oxygen enters your **lungs** and then moves into your blood.

Nutrients from food enter the blood through the **digestive system**. Your blood carries oxygen and nutrients throughout the body.

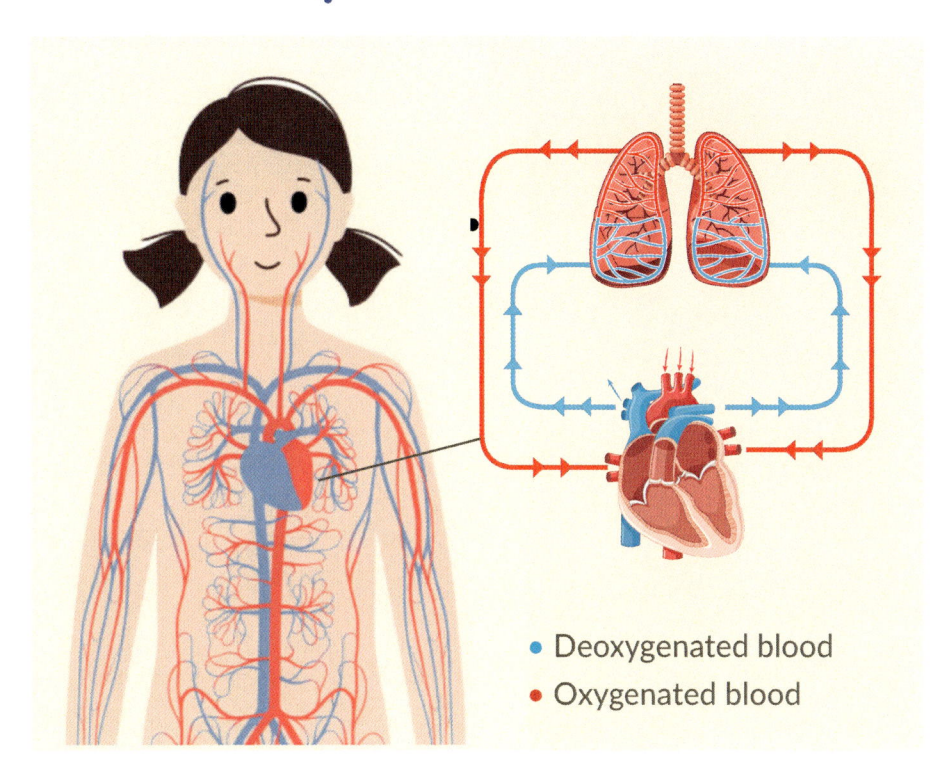

- Deoxygenated blood
- Oxygenated blood

A wide variety of foods like beets, onions, fish, citrus, and leafy greens—along with regular physical movement—help to open up your blood vessels so that your body gets extra nutrients and more oxygen.

FUN FACT!

If you were to stretch out all your blood vessels, they would extend over 60,000 miles.

Leah's Pantry Copyright | Pilot Materials

⚡ move it

Energizing Body Movements

CARDIOVASCULAR SYSTEM

① Super Squat

② Criss-cross Opener

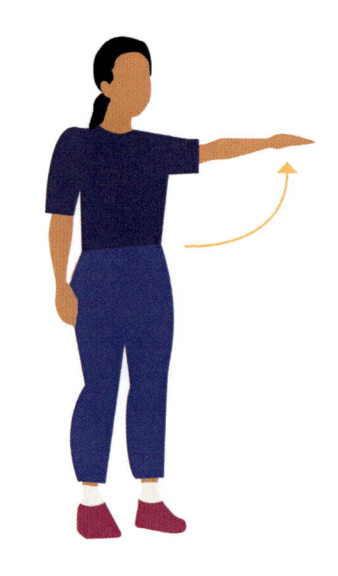

③ Power Arm Swings

Our hearts pump blood. We are a rhythm machine!

④ Raise the Roof

Leah's Pantry Copyright | Pilot Materials

Kids Body Connection

MUSCULOSKELETAL SYSTEM

Did you know that there are more than 600 muscles in your body? Your muscles are what help you move around, breathe, talk, and smile.

Important parts of the musculoskeletal system:

- Skull
- Shoulder bones
- Ribs
- Spine
- Arm and Hand Bones
- Pelvis
- Leg and Feet Bones

- muscles
- ligaments: connect bone to bone
- tendons: connect muscle to bone

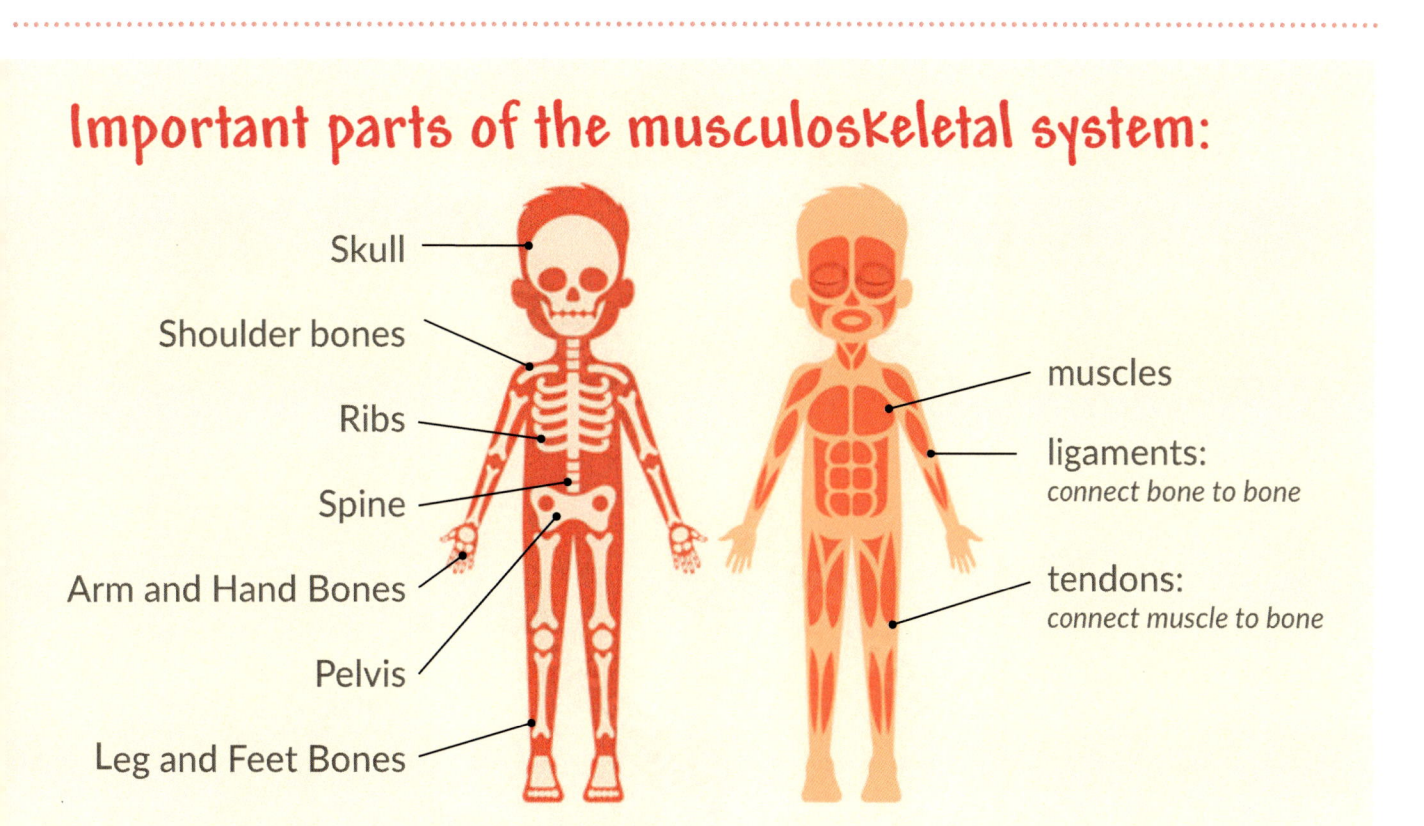

Healthy Proteins

Good sources of protein include tempeh, beans, tofu, eggs, and nuts/nut butter.

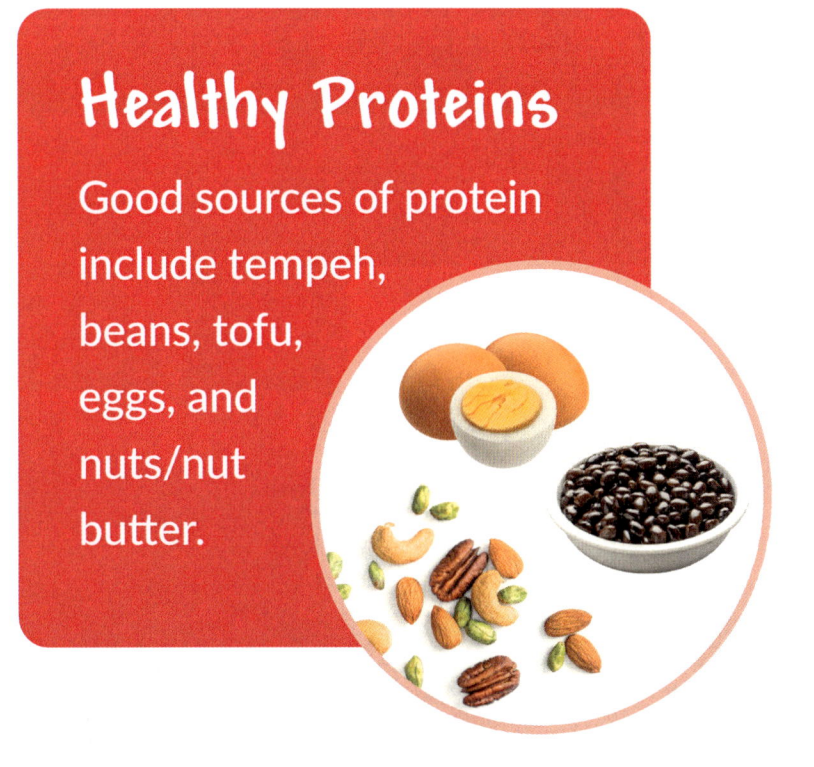

FUN FACT!

The natural curve of our spines serve as a natural shock absorber for better stability.

Leah's Pantry Copyright | Pilot Materials

⚡ move it
Movement for Strength

MUSCULOSKELETAL SYSTEM

1 Super Squats with Arm Swings

2 Shoulder Rolls

3 Walk Like an Egyptian

4 Wrist and Ankle Rolls

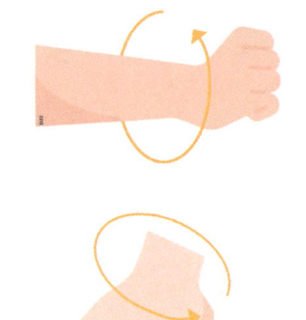

5 Leg Super Swings

6 Leg Circles

The strength of your body relies on how well the musculoskeletal system works and can affect your **flexibility**, **coordination**, and **balance**.

Leah's Pantry Copyright | Pilot Materials

Kids Body Connection

IMMUNE SYSTEM

The immune system is made up of mighty cells, tissues, and organs that join together to protect the body against diseases caused by tiny invaders, such as viruses, bacteria, and parasites. Our immune system is important for keeping us healthy.

Important parts or our immune system:

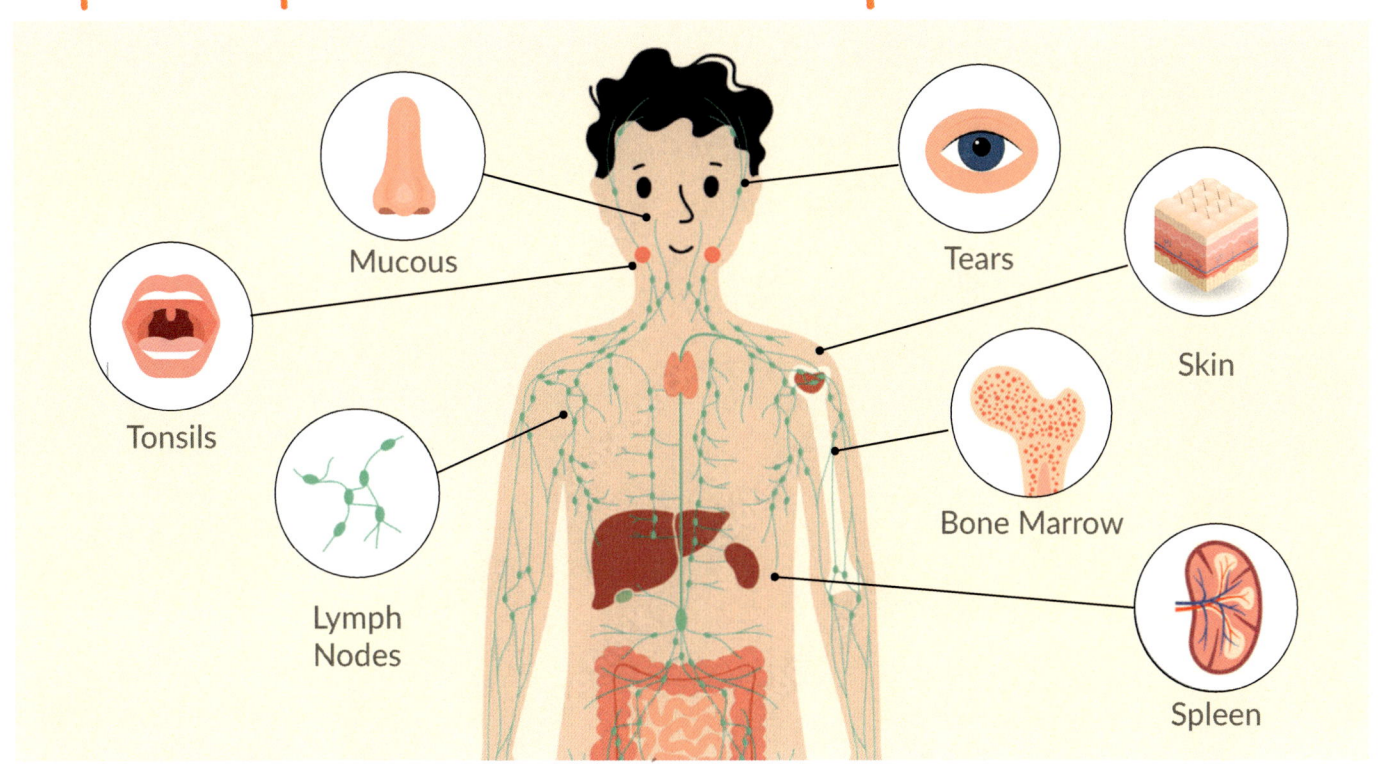

- Mucous
- Tonsils
- Lymph Nodes
- Tears
- Skin
- Bone Marrow
- Spleen

Stay Hydrated!

Drinking plenty of water supports the movement of vital body fluids and helps your body fight illness and disease.

FUN FACT!

The immune system keeps a record of every germ (microbe) it has ever defeated so it can recognize and destroy the microbe quickly if it enters the body again.

Leah's Pantry Copyright | Pilot Materials

move it
Immunity Boost

IMMUNE SYSTEM

The lymphatic system relies on **breathing**, **movement**, and **gravity** to do its work.

⬆ Bounce and swing your arms

⬇ Fold Forward

Give Yourself a Massage

BEHIND THE EAR MASSAGE

SIDE GLIDES

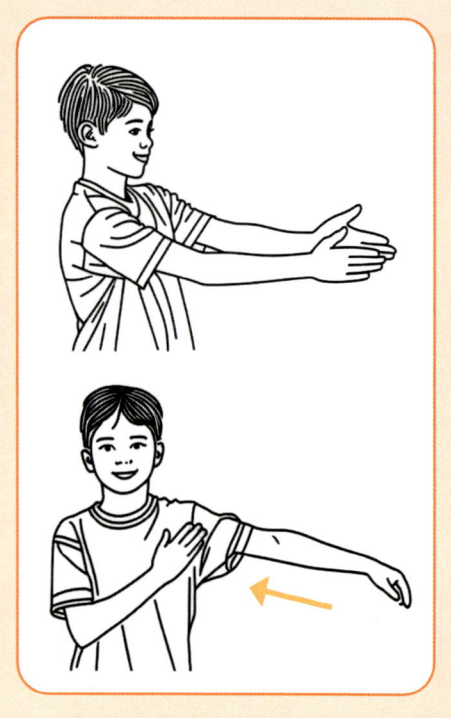

ARM GLIDES

Leah's Pantry Copyright | Pilot Materials

Kids Body Connection

DIGESTIVE SYSTEM

Your digestive system, also known as your "gut," is sometimes called the "second brain." This is because the brain and gut work together. Have you ever had the feeling of butterflies in your stomach? Those are actually signals from your brain!

What does the digestive system do?

It is the system where food gets broken down so that its energy and nutrients can be absorbed into the bloodstream.

FUN FACT!

Approximately 70-80% of our immune system is in the gut.

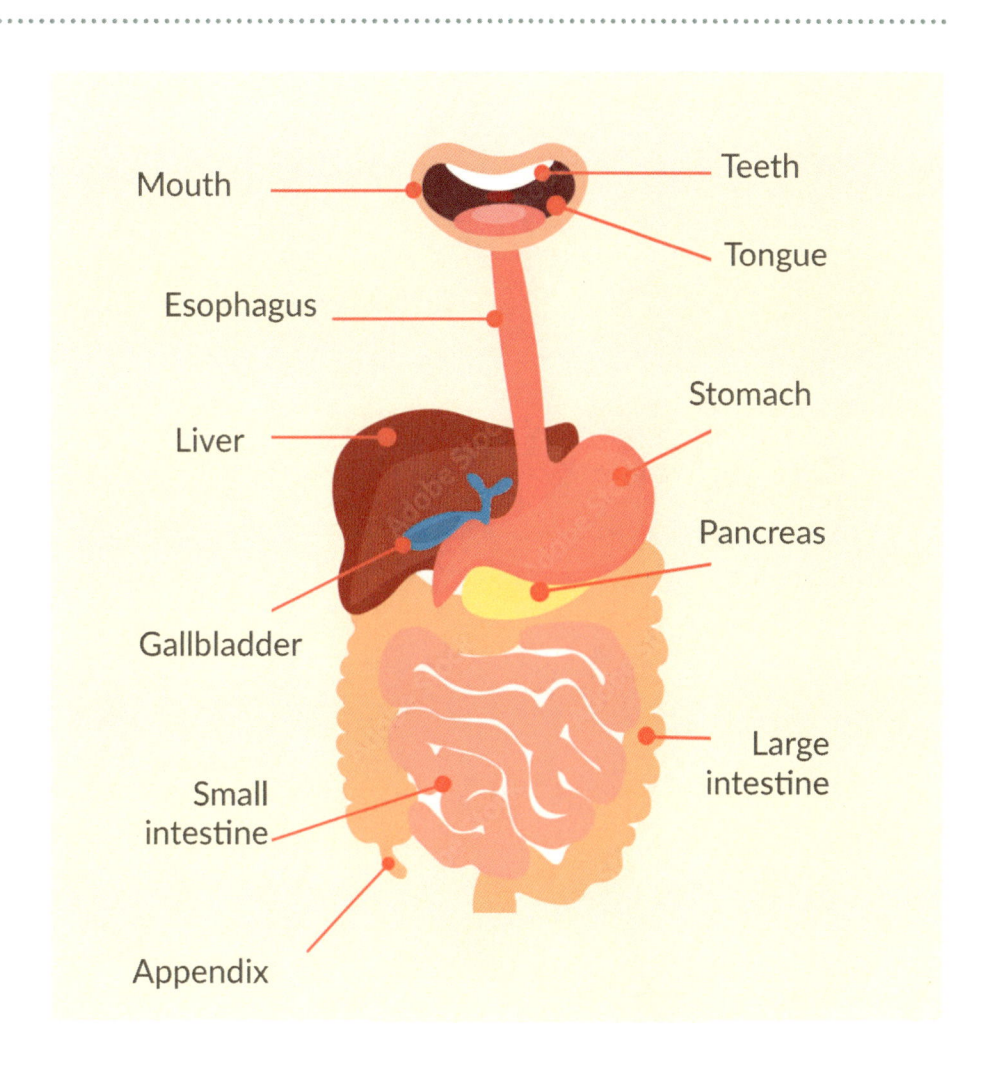

Diagram labels: Mouth, Teeth, Tongue, Esophagus, Stomach, Liver, Pancreas, Gallbladder, Small intestine, Large intestine, Appendix

Super Snacks to Try!

Hummus and veggies, popcorn, low sugar yogurt with fruit, a banana, nuts, or avocado toast.

Leah's Pantry Copyright | Pilot Materials

⚡ move it
Tummy Trouble

DIGESTIVE SYSTEM

Moving your body helps you digest food, absorb nutrients better, and can improve your mood by supporting a healthy gut-brain connection.

1 Squats

2 Let's Do the Twist

3 Belly Massage

START AT THE BOTTOM RIGHT

Leah's Pantry Copyright | Pilot Materials

What's On MyPlate? (CONTINUED)

★ What is your favorite meal? Write or draw it below.

ChooseMyPlate.gov

MyPlate

★ What does a balanced diet look like? You might be familiar with this model from the USDA. What kinds of foods fall in each category?

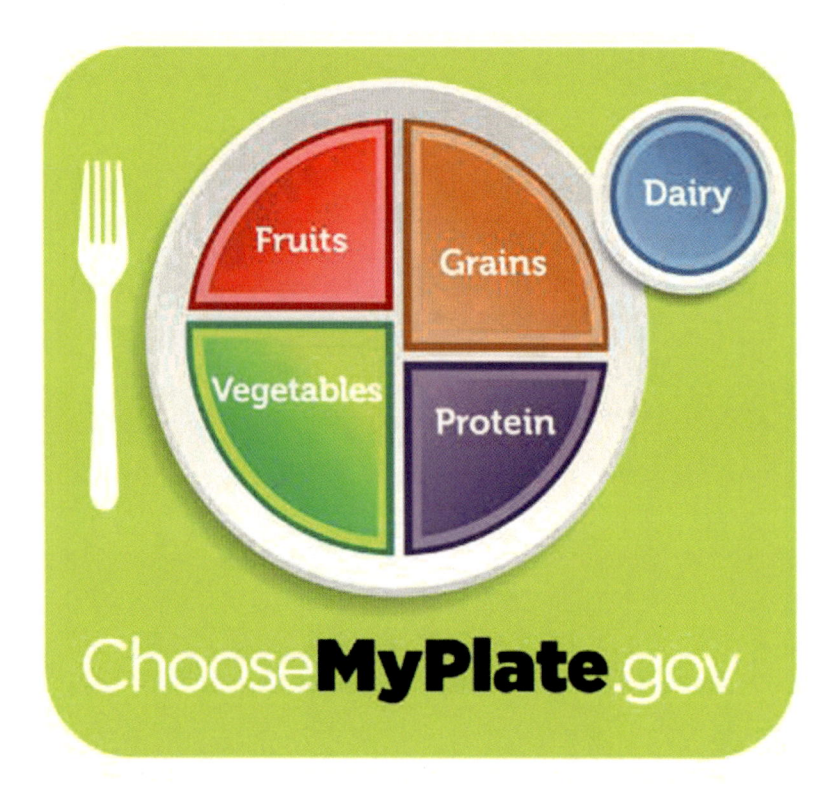

ChooseMyPlate.gov

MyPlate recommends that we:

1. Fill half our plate with fruits and vegetables.
2. Eat a different kinds of vegetables—dark green as well as other colors, leafy and starchy.
3. Eat whole fruits.
4. Make half of our grains whole grains.
5. Vary our protein sources to include beans and peas, tofu, nuts seafood, eggs, and lean meats.
6. Choose foods and beverages with less added sugars, saturated fats, and sodium.
7. Consume low-fat or fat-free dairy milk or yogurt (or fortified non-dairy versions).

» What are some ways you already or plan to follow these recommendations?

» What can be challenging for you when following these recommendations?

» How would you adapt this model to fit your culture, religious practices or food preferences?

Source: www.dietaryguidelines.gov

Healthy Eating Plate

★ Compare MyPlate to Healthy Eating Plate. How are they alike and different?

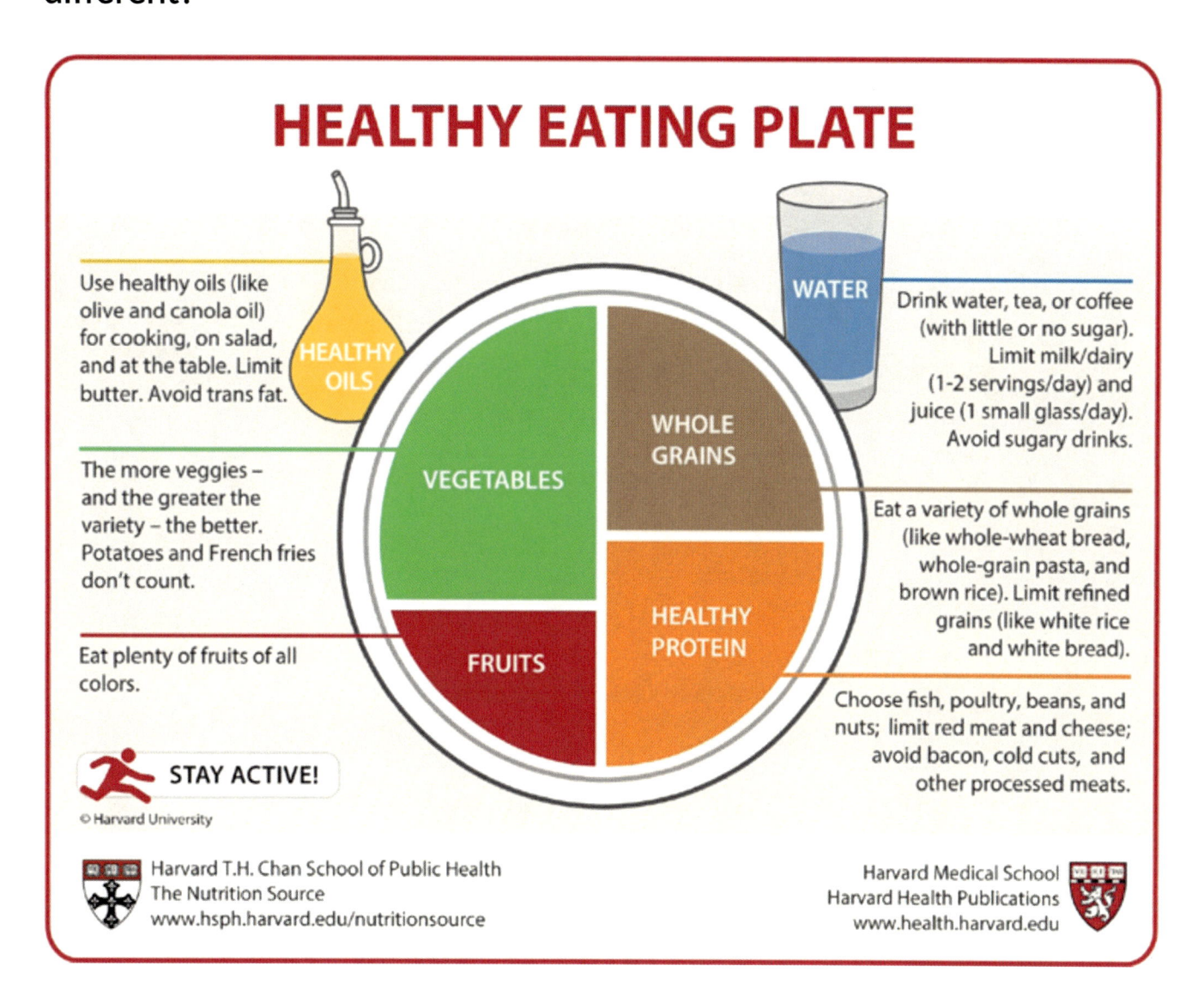

HEALTHY EATING PLATE

Use healthy oils (like olive and canola oil) for cooking, on salad, and at the table. Limit butter. Avoid trans fat.

The more veggies – and the greater the variety – the better. Potatoes and French fries don't count.

Eat plenty of fruits of all colors.

STAY ACTIVE!

© Harvard University

WATER: Drink water, tea, or coffee (with little or no sugar). Limit milk/dairy (1-2 servings/day) and juice (1 small glass/day). Avoid sugary drinks.

Eat a variety of whole grains (like whole-wheat bread, whole-grain pasta, and brown rice). Limit refined grains (like white rice and white bread).

Choose fish, poultry, beans, and nuts; limit red meat and cheese; avoid bacon, cold cuts, and other processed meats.

Harvard T.H. Chan School of Public Health
The Nutrition Source
www.hsph.harvard.edu/nutritionsource

Harvard Medical School
Harvard Health Publications
www.health.harvard.edu

Make These Meals Healthier

★ How would you make the following meals healthier? Use the guidelines of MyPlate or Healthy Eating Plate on pages 26 and 27 to help. Include more vegetables, whole grains, legumes, fruits, and dairy... and use your imagination!

Meal 1	Meal 2	Meal 3	Meal 4	Meal 5
Fried chicken White rice Salad with lettuce and cucumbers Whole milk	Hamburger on white bun French fries Milk shake	Pasta Tomato sauce Garlic bread with butter Soda	Instant Ramen Chips Juice	Stir-fry with beef and white rice

My Family's Rainbow

★ Fill in the chart with the fruits and vegetables you and your family eat the most. What colors are missing?

★ Green Foods	★ Red Foods

★ Yellow/Orange Foods	★ Blue/Purple Foods

★ White Foods	★ Others

Eat the Rainbow!

★ Which color do you eat the most? Eating a variety helps your body stay healthy.

★ **_Green Foods_**
- » Lower your chance of getting cancer
- » Keep your eyes healthy
- » Keep your bones & teeth strong

TRY IT!

spinach	kale
celery	artichokes
green beans	honeydew
broccoli	green grapes
cabbage	green apples
bok choy	limes
cucumbers	avocados
asparagus	

★ **_Yellow & Orange Foods_** 
- » Keep your heart healthy
- » Keep your eyes healthy
- » Lower your chance of getting cancer
- » Keep you from catching colds

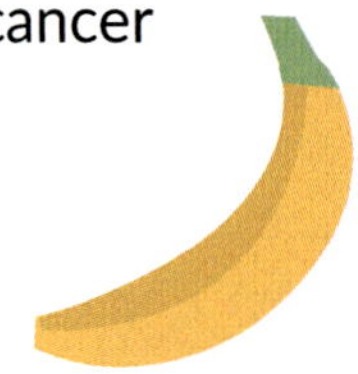

TRY IT!

carrots	cantaloupe
sweet potatoes	tangerines
yellow peppers	mangoes
pumpkins	oranges
pineapple	lemons
papayas	peaches

★ **_Red Foods_**
- » Keep your heart healthy 
- » Keep your bladder healthy
- » Keep your memory strong
- » Lower your chance of getting cancer

TRY IT!

tomatoes	watermelon
red peppers	red onion
red cabbage	red apples
strawberries	beets
cherries	

★ **_Blue & Purple Foods_** 
- » Stay healthy when you get old
- » Keep your memory strong
- » Keep your bladder healthy
- » Lower your chance of getting cancer

TRY IT!

eggplant	blueberries
purple cabbage	blackberries
raisins	purple grapes

★ **_White Foods_**
- » Keep your heart healthy
- » Have good cholesterol levels
- » Lower your chance of getting cancer

TRY IT!

onion	ginger
green onion	garlic
cauliflower	jicama
chives	fennel
mushrooms	

Make Half Your Grains Whole

★ Why choose whole grains?

Whole grains are usually darker in color and stronger in flavor than refined grains and flours. Eating whole grains has been shown to lower the risk for diabetes, heart disease, high cholesterol, and high blood pressure.

A whole grain contains the germ, endosperm and bran, while a refined or processed grain only contains the endosperm. The germ and bran are the most nutrient rich parts of the grain, and the highest in fiber. Check the ingredient list to make sure you're getting a truly whole grain product: the first ingredient should be something like "whole wheat" and not just "wheat."

Sometimes whole grains can be identified with this stamp:

REFINED GRAIN FOODS
(endosperm only)
- White pasta
- White bread
- Most cakes, cookies, and pastries

WHOLE GRAINS
(bran + endosperm + germ)
- Oats
- Brown rice
- Whole wheat
- Barley
- Buckwheat
- Farro
- Spelt
- Quinoa
- Millet
- Teff

Bran: protects the seed
- Fiber
- B vitamins
- Minerals

Endosperm: energy for the seed
- Carbohydrates
- Some protein
- Some B vitamins

Germ: nourishment for the seed
- B vitamins
- Vitamin E
- Minerals
- Phytochemicals

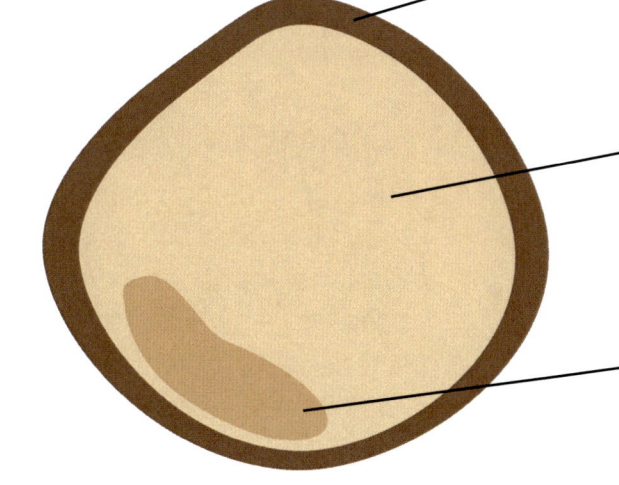

DID YOU KNOW?

A diet rich in fiber, as found in whole grains and beans, helps your digestion and keeps you full for longer. Make sure to get 3 servings of whole grains and 4½ cups of fruits and veggies each day for the recommended amount of fiber.

Grain Game

★ Can you identify different whole grains?

Grains have been an important source of energy for thousands of years. Whole or unrefined grains that contain all parts of the seed provide important nutrients such as fiber, minerals, healthy fats, disease-fighting antioxidants, and several are a good source of complete protein. Can you match the grain with its description? Write the number next to the definition.

- __ **AMARANTH**, an ancient grain that was cultivated in South America since about 8000 years ago. Amaranth has a peppery taste with a pleasantly sweet, grassy aroma. It's tiny grains can be prepared in porridge or polenta style recipes. It can also be popped like popcorn!

- __ **BARLEY** is one of the world's earliest grains from Ancient China to Europe and Africa. It was even a food for gladiators (who mostly ate a vegetarian diet!). To be sure you are getting the best nutrition, look for barley labeled as whole, hulled, or hull-less. You might have had barley in soup but it makes a good substitute for rice in many dishes.

- __ **BROWN RICE** is a whole grain while white rice is not. Brown rice contains double the nutrition as refined white rice. Other whole grain rice can be black, purple, or red. Wild rice is not actually rice but is also very nutritious and flavorful.

- __ **BUCKWHEAT** is not a type of wheat—in fact it's not technically a grain at all but is used just like one! Buckwheat has a strong flavor. Buckwheat flour is used for traditional noodles like Japanese soba while cracked buckwheat makes a good hot porridge.

- __ **BULGUR WHEAT** is produced when whole wheat kernels are cleaned, boiled, dried, and grounded. It needs to be boiled for only about 10 minutes to be ready to eat, making it great for side dishes, pilafs, or salads. Middle Eastern tabbouleh is a famous salad prepared with bulgur.

- __ **CORN** is more than just sweet corn that we enjoy with butter and salt. Popcorn is a type of flint corn grown by Indigenous Americans. It's a delicious whole grain snack. Dried field corn kernels, also called hominy, can be used in soups or side dishes. Masa, a ground hominy dough, is used to make corn tortillas. Ground hominy corn is also used to make porridges like grits and polenta.

- __ **MILLET** is mentioned in Ancient Greek and Ancient Roman texts and was common in Medieval Europe. It can be used to make sweet or savory porridges, baked goods and flat breads in Indian and Ethiopian cuisine.

- __ **OATS** have been around since the earliest humans! Whether they are rolled or steel cut, oats are almost always in their whole grain form. They are good breakfast foods because oats keep you full longer. Oats can also be used in savory dishes like jook/congee or risotto.

■ Cooking Tip

Whole grain kernels can be cooked like rice but may require differing amounts of water or cooking time. Most can be used as a substitute when rice is called for in sweet or savory recipes. Or if you are still getting used to eating whole grains, mix some into your white rice to improve its nourishment.

[continues on next page...]

Grain Game (CONTINUED)

__ **QUINOA** is not exactly a grain, but these tiny kernels can be eaten like one. In fact, it is actually related to spinach! It was sacred to the Ancient Mayans who considered it "the mother of all grains." Quinoa cooks quickly and is delicious in warm and cold grain salads and as a side dish.

__ **WHEAT BERRIES** are the individual wheat kernels that can be cooked like rice to be enjoyed as a side dish. Red wheat berries are produced from a modern wheat plant. Spelt and farro are a type of wheat berry are more similar to what was first grown by humans over 10,000 years ago!

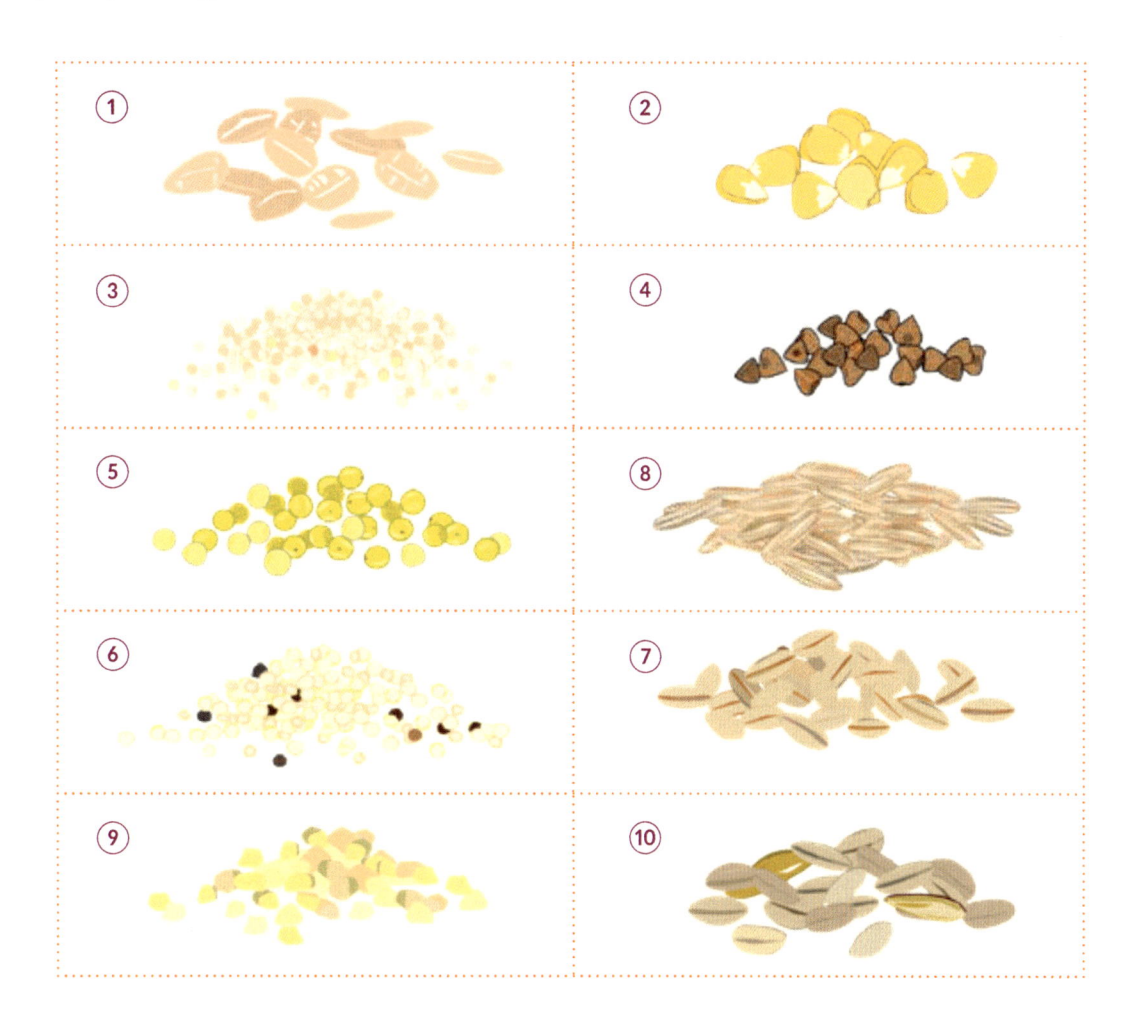

Answers: 1. Oats, 2. Corn, 3. Amarant, 4. Buckwheat, 5. Millet, 6. Quinoa, 7. Wheat berries, 8. Brown rice, 9. Bulgur wheat, 10. Barley.

Bean Game

★ What beans do you know?

Beans contain nutrients—especially protein and fiber—that we need to heal our bodies, prevent heart disease and cancer, support digestion, and build new muscle, bone, hair, teeth and blood. They have been an important part of cuisines around the world for thousands of years. Can you match the bean with its description? Write the number next to the definition.

__ **SOY BEANS** originated from Asia and commonly used to make many delicious foods and drinks like soy milk, tofu, tempeh, soybean oil, and many vegetarian options. Have you ever had edamame? They cook quickly and have a sweet, buttery flavor..

__ **CHICKPEAS (or GARBANZO BEANS)** have a nutty buttery flavor and creamy texture. They are very common in middle eastern, Mediterranean, Indian, Spanish and French cooking, but are also found in many cuisines around the world. They can be ground up or pureed to make falafel and hummus. Cooked whole chickpeas are great in salads and stews.

__ **BLACK BEANS** are sweet-tasting with a soft texture. They are popular in Central American, South American, and Caribbean cuisine. Black beans and rice is a common dish that goes by names such as Congrí, Moros y Christianos, and Casamiento in Spanish-speaking countries.

__ **SPLIT PEAS** are dried field peas (green peas are a type of young field pea). Yellow or green split peas are commonly used to make soups around the world—Green Split Pea (North America & Europe), Dal (India), and Tamaraqt (Morocco). In fact, the Greeks and Romans were making split pea soup since at least 500 B.C.

__ **KIDNEY BEANS** have a firm texture, and are a great addition to salads. They also hold up well in soups and stews like American chili, or other dishes that cook for a long time. Light red kidney beans are popular in the Caribbean region, Portugal, and Spain.

__ **SMALL RED BEANS** have a more delicate flavor and softer texture compared to kidney beans. Small red beans are particularly popular in the Caribbean region, where they traditionally are eaten with rice. Small red beans are also used to make Louisiana Red Beans & Rice.

__ **LENTILS** come in a wide variety of colors, sizes and textures. Some varieties are red, brown, blue-green, yellow, or black. The term lentil comes from the word for lens, which describes the shape of these legumes. Lentils are an ancient food- Archaeologists found evidence of lentils in Greek ruins from 11,000 B.C!

▎ Cooking Tip

If you are using dried beans, rinse and pick through before preparing. Many beans should be soaked before cooking to shorten the cooking time and make them more tender. Cooking time depends on the variety. Do not use any salt or acidic ingredients while cooking. Canned beans can be rinsed to reduce the sodium content.

[continues on next page...]

Bean Game (CONTINUED)

___ **BLACK-EYED PEAS** have an earthy, nutty taste. They originated in West Africa and were introduced to the Americas by enslaved people. Hoppin' John is a soul food tradition that is meant to bring good luck for the New Year. Middle Eastern, Asian, Indian, Caribbean, South American, and European cultures also use black-eyed peas.

___ **PINTO BEANS** got their name from the Spanish word for "speckled," but they lose their spotted appearance when cooked. Pinto beans are the most widely produced bean in the U.S. and are used to make Mexican refried beans.

___ **NAVY BEANS** have a mild, delicate flavor. These are the beans used in Boston Baked Beans. These white beans were named Navy Beans because they were fed to sailors in the U.S. Navy in the 1800's.

Answers: 1. Pinto beans, 2. Lentils, 3. Split peas, 4. Black beans, 5. Small red beans, 6. Soy beans, 7. Kidney beans, 8. Black-eyed peas, 9. Navy beans, 10. Chickpeas.

Rethink Your Drink

★ **How much sugar is in your favorite drink? Use the nutrition facts to find out.**

» Use the nutrition facts to find out.
» Check the number of servings per container. Will you drink more than one?
» For each serving, do the math: grams of sugar ÷ 4 = teaspoons of sugar
   For example: 40g sugar ÷ 4 = 10 teaspoons sugar

TRY IT! Now do the math on these other soft drinks. How many teaspoons of sugar in each serving? In each bottle or can?

ORANGE SODA
Nutrition Facts
Serving Size 8 oz.
Servings per Container 2

Amount per Serving

Calories 168   Calories from Fat 0

Total Fat 0g
   Saturated Fat 0g
   Trans Fat 0g
Cholesterol 0mg
Sodium 50mg
Total Carbohydrate 42g
   Dietary Fiber 0g
   Sugars 42g
Protein 0g

Vitamin D 0%   Calcium 0%
Potassium 0%   Iron 0%

CHOCOLATE MILK
Nutrition Facts
Serving Size 8 oz.
Servings per Container 1

Amount per Serving

Calories 193   Calories from Fat 81

Total Fat 9g
   Saturated Fat 5g
   Trans Fat 0g
Cholesterol 35mg
Sodium 125mg
Total Carbohydrate 20g
   Dietary Fiber 0g
   Sugars 20g
Protein 8g

Vitamin D 15%   Calcium 25%
Potassium 10%   Iron 0%

SWEET TEA
Nutrition Facts
Serving Size 8 oz.
Servings per Container 3

Amount per Serving

Calories 144   Calories from Fat 0

Total Fat 0g
   Saturated Fat 0g
   Trans Fat 0g
Cholesterol 0mg
Sodium 50mg
Total Carbohydrate 36g
   Dietary Fiber 0g
   Sugars 36g
Protein 0g

Vitamin D 0%   Calcium 0%
Potassium 0%   Iron 0%

COLA
Nutrition Facts
Serving Size 1 can (12 fl. oz.)
Servings per Container 1

Amount per Serving

Calories 150   Calories from Fat 0

Total Fat 0g
   Saturated Fat 0g
   Trans Fat 0g
Cholesterol 0mg
Sodium 50mg
Total Carbohydrate 40g
   Dietary Fiber 0g
   Sugars 40g
Protein 0g

Vitamin A 0%   Vitamin C 0%
Iron 0%   Iron 0%   Calcium 0%

Rethink Your Drink (CONTINUED)

★ Drink Water Instead!

- » Add lemon to your water for extra flavor. Or try the recipe below.
- » Try drinking hot, cold, and room temperature water to see what you like best.
- » Have a glass of water on the table at every meal, and nearby when working.
- » Drink a glass in the morning after waking up.
- » Drink water instead of snacking.
- » Drink water when you eat out. It's free!
- » Note that in many places, tap water must meet many more standards than bottled water! Bottled water also sits in plastic. This may be harmful to human health and the Earth. Consider saving money and drinking local tap water from a reusable glass or metal bottle.

★ Flavored Water Recipe

Fill a pitcher with cool water.

Add ½ cup thinly sliced cucumber and ½ cup fresh mint leaves. Chill in refrigerator. Enjoy!

Try different combinations of flavors:

- » Thin slices: lemon, lime, orange, grapefruit, cucumber, apple, berries, melon, pineapple, fresh ginger
- » Fresh whole leaves or sprigs: mint, basil, rosemary, parsley

Don't Call Me Sugar!

★ There are many names for the sugar added to food. Can you find the ones hidden here?

- BARLEY MALT
- BROWN SUGAR
- CANE JUICE
- CORN SYRUP
- DEXTRIN
- DEXTROSE
- FRUCTOSE
- GLUCOSE
- HONEY
- LACTOSE
- MALTOSE
- MAPLE SYRUP
- MOLASSES
- SWEETENER

```
H O N E Y F E M A T R A P S A
M E N U K S W E E T E N E R N
T A N I R A H C C A S E H F A
U R R S O R B I T O L O M R Y
R N I R T X E D C R A C A U W
G A S M M E E O J I S L P C T
L I G R B A R L E Y M A L T E
U E T U Y N M X Q O E C E O E
C S E S S A L O M S E T S S W
O U L Y L N K L O T L O Y E S
S O R T H Y W R E T C S R B A
E U O D H T T O O N L E U H R
P S T P G X V Z R T U P P F T
E T C M E W B C A B D M G A U
S T R D B C A N E J U I C E N
```

BONUS Can you find these artificial sweeteners too? These are chemicals with few or no calories.
ASPARTAME   NUTRASWEET   SACCHARIN   SORBITOL